Finding Stoney

Sue Skelding

Finding Stoney

by Sue Skelding

Copyright 2024   Sue Skelding
First Edition

Cover Credit:
Sue Skelding Books, LLC

For Worldwide Distribution
Printed in the U.S.A.

1

Ernest, Liam, and I were making our way back to the barn after intercepting Sullivan, the naughty, cat-chasing Golden Doodle who had come within inches of being hit by a passing truck on the busy road in front of Mrs. Rae's house. We had already had quite an eventful morning rescuing a runaway pinto, and after our little dog chase, I was looking forward to a peaceful afternoon.

"Race you!" Liam said.

Just as I was about to launch forward, Mrs. Rae's white Honda pulled in the driveway. When she parked, Ernest jogged over to help Grandpa Joe get out of the passenger seat. Mom exited the barn and joined Liam and me. We quickly headed towards the vehicle.

"Sullivan's on a leash?" Mrs. Rae inquired. "Let me guess; he did the naughty cat chase."

Liam and I could only nod. We were tired, thirsty, and long past hungry.

Mrs. Rae leaned against the door on the driver's side. She looked as hot and tired as we all were. "When I got to the ice cream store, I found Grandpa Joe struggling to breath. He tried using the inhaler that I brought him, but after a couple of treatments without improvement, I insisted he come home where there is less smoke in the air."

"Good idea," Mom said. "Our Grandpa Jake also has asthma and smoldering—anything immediately causes him distress."

Mrs. Rae eyed the truck Mom had driven to her farm. "I see you finished parking and unhitching the horse trailer. I appreciate everything you and your family have done for me already, but I'm hoping you can help me a while longer. Is there any way you could stay with Grandpa Joe while I close up the ice cream store and check on the Fagan barn? A lady from the cheese shop next to Grandpa's place is watching it for me while I drove him home." She giggled. "The only way I could get the old goat to leave the delicatessen was to promise I would go check on his granddad's boat. I tried telling him the Fagan fire was only in the farmhouse's breezeway and had nothing to do with the barns, but he refused to budge unless I promised."

Mom raised an eyebrow—a talent only she and Liam possessed. "Then why is there still so much smoke in downtown Aloha?"

For a second, her question baffled me. Just like Liam, I sometimes mixed up *Aloha*, the pony name with *Aloha*, the town name. I knew the difference was in the way they are pronounced, but it was still easy to get confused.

Mrs. Rae checked the time. She was wearing a fancy new iPhone watch that receives emails and incoming texts. "The property that was on fire this morning isn't what's currently burning and filling the air with black smoke. It's the old fish hatchery located halfway between Aloha and Cheboygan. However, on the way here, I heard on the radio that fire is also now under control."

Ernest and Liam cackled loudly at something Grandpa Joe said.

Mrs. Rae, Mom, and I looked up in time to see Liam and Ernest helping the elderly man up the stairs. Each boy was assisting Grandpa Joe at his side. Mrs. Rae opened her car door and reached in and nabbed Grandpa Joe's cane.

"Mia," she said, handing me the sturdy piece of driftwood. "Would you mind taking this to Grandpa Joe? It's difficult for him to navigate without it."

I gave Mrs. Rae the coiled lunge line that Sullivan was attached to, and she placed the antique cane in my open palm.

The instant the wood touched my skin, my heart skipped a beat. I remem-  bered first spying Grandpa Joe's inscribed cane earlier that day as Liam and I were leaving the ice cream store. I had immediately wanted to know more about its history, but we didn't have time. Now, as I held the knotty twirls tightly in my left hand, I delicately ran my fingers across the etched letters that had been artfully burnt into the decaying wood. I momentarily held my breath and paused. I wished for the vintage cane to transfer its story to me. I wanted to feel its magic like I thought I had experienced when I placed my hands on the tamarack tree at Tahquamenon Falls when were searching for the Spirit Bear last summer.

"Lady Aloha" has to mean something important to be carved into Grandpa Joe's cane. How does the metallic object Liam found at the bottom of Mullett Lake fit into the puzzle? I yearned to know more, but I knew the timing wasn't right. Mom and Dad had taught Liam and me to be polite, and this was one of those moments when I knew better than to bring it up.

The closer I got to Ernest, Liam, and Grandpa Joe, my mind sizzled with questions. When I heard them discussing sturgeon fishing on Mullett Lake, any hope I had of gleaning even the tiniest fact about *Lady Aloha* diminished.

We settled Grandpa Joe at the kitchen table. Ernest opened the refrigerator door and pulled out four ice-cold bottles of water. He handed one to Liam before setting the other three on the table. Liam pulled the centerpiece candy dish closer. "Grandpa Joe loves Mackinac Island saltwater taffy," Ernest said.

"So does my dad," Liam chimed in.

Grandpa removed his wide-brimmed fishing hat and put it in his lap. When Ernest went to sit in the chair beside him, Grandpa Joe tapped Ernest's wrist and said, "Go with your Auntie to lock up the ice cream store. On the way there, make sure she stops at the Fagan farm. I know she said the first fire wasn't anywhere near the old barn, but I want you to personally check on it for me. Since I can't be there, I need you to be my eyes, Son." His voice began sounding more hoarse and tired. "Promise you'll open up the big barn door and go inside. Touch my beauty and make sure she is safe."

Ernest stood close to his grandfather. "I'm sure it's fine, Grandpa. You shouldn't be alone. Someone needs to stay with you."

Grandpa Joe walloped the corner of the chair with his cane. "Go on, now! Tell your auntie I said you're going! I'll be just fine."

Ernest peered first at Liam, and then at me.

"Come on!" he urged.

2

On the way outside, I tagged close behind Ernest and Liam. I considered offering to stay back with Grandpa Joe so he wouldn't be alone, but I knew Mom wouldn't want me to be by myself if something happened. Once, when I was younger, I had seen my Grandpa Jake have an asthma attack that really scared me. He had coughed so hard his face practically turned blue.

Mom and Mrs. Rae were still standing next to the white car. Liam's spindly legs got him there faster than Ernest and me.

Mrs. Rae handed Sullivan's lead to Ernest and was about to say something when Ernest interjected, "Grandpa Joe is insisting I go with you to the store, so I can personally check on his boat. He wants me to open the barn doors and inspect the hull."

Mrs. Rae shook her head. "I should have known. That's fine. Pile in the car, kids."

Mom brushed her sweaty hands against her shorts. It was hot, and I was sure she had to be thirsty. "I'll stay with Ernest's grandpa," she said. "That way I'll be able to use the landline to phone Mrs. Davidson and check on Aurora; she's probably wondering where her truck is. I will also call your Dad and explain we will be a little longer. No worry there though; he and Mr. Davidson are probably still out on Mullett lake fishing."

"What about Sullivan?" Ernest asked, peering up at his aunt's face.

Mrs. Rae giggled. "Bring him along. The more the merrier."

I thought Sullivan's being able to ride along with us might make Liam happy as he loved dogs, but I could tell something was bothering him. I quietly whispered, "Is something the matter?"

Liam shrugged his shoulders, and Mom noticed. "What's wrong, Liam?"

Then it occurred to me that we hadn't checked on Bently. "Are you worried about your piglet?"

Mom hugged Liam. "Don't give it another thought. I'll make sure he is okay. Go have fun and remember above all else, use common sense."

3

I climbed into the front seat and before buckling in, I turned and gave Sullivan a big pat on his curly head. His overzealous excitement at being allowed in the vehicle was beyond hilarious. Both Ernest and Liam were desperately trying to put on their seatbelts, but the second they quit protecting themselves from Sullivan's monster-long tongue, he'd swipe a slobbery kiss across their faces.

"Gross," Ernest cried out. "His tongue went in my mouth."

"Sullivan!" Mrs. Rae sternly said. Then she shrieked, "No! Don't do that! Not in my ear!"

Since the vehicle was still in park, I unclipped, turned with my knees on the seat, and snagged Sullivan by his leather collar. I held on tightly while the boys got settled. The smooth texture reminded me of Mom's rolled leather show bridle that she has had since she was a little girl.

 She found it not too long ago when she was hunting for something in an old tack box. She said it had been her first big purchase when she was ten years old. She recalled earning the money to buy it from riding and training a younger girl's pony in the stable. Show bridles are different now; the straps are commonly flat but in dressage and saddle-seat, sometimes the browbands are accented with different colors or even bejeweled.

After the boys were finally strapped in, I released the lick-o-maniac Sullivan. Then I buckled in, and Mrs. Rae put the car in reverse. Sullivan's heavy panting instantly heated up the inside of the vehicle, and we all lowered our windows a crack until the air conditioner caught up.

Mrs. Rae checked her watch again. "It won't take me very long to close up the ice cream store. I would ask you kids to come inside and help, but the rowdy way Sullivan's acting it seems a little dangerous." She glanced at her mischievous pooch in the rearview mirror and smiled lovingly.

Ernest was sitting in the backseat directly behind me, and because he periodically kicked the back of my seat, I surmised he was still struggling to hold off the enthusiastic dog.

"Aunt Cathy, the way Sullivan's acting, is it possible to drop off Liam, Mia, and me at the Fagan farm on the way to Grandpa's store? That way we can check on the boat while you're closing down the shop. It will also give this loose-lipped mutt something to occupy his tongue. He's crazy today!"

We all laughed, but I could hear the frustration in Ernest's voice.

Since I was sitting in the front seat next to Mrs. Rae, I could see her lip slightly curl, and I wondered if she was thinking about saying "No." When Dad makes that face, Liam and I know he will usually respond with one word: "Doubtful."

"Please, Aunt Cathy. We'll only go into the big, red barn. You said the fire wasn't anywhere near it, and besides, the driveway to the farmhouse is a long way away."

Sullivan must have known he was being talked about. He let out a giant "woof!"

"He's a character," I said.

Mrs. Rae rolled her eyes and then nodded. "Okay," she said. "Only on one condition! Stay away from the Fagan house, and don't bother the renters who are living on the other side of the property near the abandoned stables."

"Abandoned stables?" *Why would anyone desert a horse barn?*

Ernest pushed Sullivan onto Liam's lap so he could lean forward. "Grandpa Joe said those renters left six weeks ago. He said he couldn't believe they up and moved in the middle of the night. He also said he wasn't happy because evidently they left several cats to fend for themselves."

Mrs. Rae retrieved her cell phone from her pocket. "I'll bet that's why I overheard Grandpa questioning his friend about a live animal trap. I meant to ask him about it back then, but I got distracted doing something else. Here, Ernest. Take Grandpa Joe's phone. He left it in my car. If you have any problems, call me at the shop. Otherwise, I'll be back within the hour."

As Ernest reached for the cellphone, of course Sullivan bumped his hand, and the device landed on the seat next to me.

"Mia, why don't you keep the phone in your pocket since it appears Ernest and Liam have their hands full."

Lots of pets have come to Mom's veterinary hospital, but I wasn't sure I had ever seen such a happy dog before. I suppose it's what she means when she says, "She'll take a bouncing, cra-cra puppy any day rather than an aggressive dog."

Moments later, our car slowed, and I heard the blinker click right before we turned. Wilting yellow-and-brown grass stalks lined the driveway, and if it weren't for the two tall sliding barn doors directly in front of us, discerning this was a driveway would have been impossible.

To our right was an overgrown front yard that appeared to go with the dilapidated, two-story house a short distance away. Pieces of butter-yellow siding hung loosely, and the porch railing dangled dangerously across the front. Large, muddy tire tracks led from the side of the house up a deeply rutted driveway. Yellow police tape secured the area.

From where I was sitting in the passenger's seat, seeing the rental house and empty stables located on the other side of the driveway was impossible.

"What happened to the horse barn next door?

Why isn't it being used? Why would anyone let something like that go?"

Mrs. Rae coasted to a stop. She took a deep breath, then explained twenty years ago the standardbred and thoroughbred horse racing industry took a huge hit, and as a result, Michigan business owners terminated several tracks. "Those closures left many horse owners with too many horses to feed when no money was coming in. That was a very sad time. Many horses suffered, and people lost their farms that had been in their family for generations. Okay," she said. "Jump out and be careful! Call me if you need anything."

4

Mrs. Rae's explanation left me feeling dismal. I remembered Mom telling me about the closures when she had explained the origin of the dam (the female parent) of her rambunctious, young thoroughbred, "Foolish."

Sullivan, Liam, and Ernest ran full tilt toward the big red barn.

Sullivan, in his glory, leaped over a small rock as if it were a tall stone wall. Bumblebees buzzed in the assortment of blue, yellow, and red wildflowers sparsely populating the dried overgrowth in front of the structure.

Ernest held Sullivan close to his side as Liam tried to slide open the weathered wooden door. Even with putting all his weight behind it, the door wouldn't budge.

"Let me try," Ernest said, handing Sullivan's leash to me.

Just like with Liam, the stubborn door remained securely closed.

"I don't get it," Ernest said. "Grandpa just hooks his cane around the end of it near the center and then gives the door a big shove with his foot."

Sullivan whined; he wanted in. Or rather, he "wanted" something—anything.

"Just wait, Sullivan, you big baby! You're as spoiled as Aloha. No wonder the two of you are best friends." I patted Sullivan playfully on his head. "Boys. I have an idea." I waited for Liam to roll his eyes, but he never did. "Ernest, since you are closest to the front portion of the slider, when I say "go," pull the door out toward your body. While you do that, Liam and I will push it as hard as we can to the right."

Ernest looked confused, but he nodded. "If you say so." He wrapped his fingers around the edge of the splintering wood and said, "I'm ready."

I peered at Liam to make sure he understood. "Okay. 1, 2, 3, go!"

Like I was a wizard, the weathered wooden door slid to the east with so much zest, it threw Liam to the ground.

Ernest turned and stared at me. "How'd you know to do that," he asked.

I grinned. I secretly liked being thought of as *smart*. Liam was normally the quick thinker in the family.

"When you said Grandpa Joe hooks his cane on the end of the door before he pushes it sideways, I figured the curved end on his cane probably pulled the door outward, making it easier to slide."

Liam glanced up toward the top of the warped door. "The sliding mechanism is rusty, and I'll bet the trolly is a little bent."

Ernst cackled, "Probably from when Grandpa Joe banged into it the last time he backed in his grandpa's boat. Wait until you see how big she is."

Even with the front door slid wide open, initially it was too dark to clearly see inside. While I waited for my eyes to adjust, I appreciated the scent of aging wood and the creaks and groans of a hundred-year-old barn. Streaks of light sifted through tiny gaps between the planks.

Slowly, like a curtain raising in a movie theatre, my vision improved. When it finally cleared, sitting smack in front of me was a majestic wonder.

Sullivan tugged Ernest to the far side of the barn, and I heard him tell the playful pooch to settle down.

"Isn't my great-grandpa's boat a beauty?" Ernest asked. "Fifty-eight feet of polished mahogany with a 16-foot beam (the width of vessel at the widest point). That's as wide as they are allowed to be to fit through the Cheboygan locks that lead to Lake Huron."

Liam could only nod in awe. I was positive he had never seen a wooden boat of this magnitude, and he appeared to be as captivated by the sight as I was.

A thought suddenly occurred to  me. *Ernest called the boat a "she" like Dad and Mr. Davidson had talked about the boat we took fish-ing.* "You too?!" I stammered. "Why does everyone assume boats are females?"

Ernest's giant smile could have lit up the barn when he held out his arm and said, "Let me introduce you to *Lady*..."

He didn't have time to finish his sentence. Sullivan suddenly woofed playfully, followed by a sharp yip, yip, yip! Like a racehorse leaving the starting gate, Sullivan lunged forward, face-planting Ernest on the uneven barn floor.

Twenty-five feet of lunge line slowly snaked through Ernest's fingers moments before we heard an ear-piercing cat scream that sent shivers up my spine. *Sullivan is on the chase.*

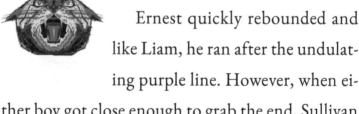 Ernest quickly rebounded and like Liam, he ran after the undulating purple line. However, when either boy got close enough to grab the end, Sullivan darted in the opposite direction, flipping the loop out of their grasp.

I instinctively bolted to the front barn door to slide it closed. At Mom's veterinary hospital the first thing any of her employees shouted when a cat or dog escapes their hold was, "Shut the doors!" Mom had explained that's why veterinary clinics have so many doors between the interior of the building and the exit.

After accomplishing my objective, I took a deep breath and slowly turned around. I knew our cat-chasing, bad-boy doodle was trapped. *All we have to do is catch the end of his leash and reel him in like a fish on a line.*

Unfortunately, closing the front door temporarily darkened the interior of the barn. I waited for my eyes to adjust to the lack of light before stepping forward. I heard rustling toward the rear of the barn and then the sounds of cans falling off shelves and crashing to the floor.

Ernest screamed, "Sullivan, stop!"

Then Liam shouted, "No! Sullivan. Please don't do that!"

I darted around the giant mahogany vessel in time to see Liam hurling like a linebacker toward the rear barn wall. It wasn't until I had completely made it around the hull that I discovered why Liam had done a bellyflop.

With the front barn door wide open, natural light had flooded in, lighting the interior. All the cracks and imperfections in the building's exterior had somehow been disguised. Closing the heavy slider had revealed a bear-sized hole near the ground on the rear wall.

The opening had beckoned the terrified tabby and Sullivan to shoot through to freedom.

Liam and I reacted faster than Ernest. We ran to the opening and dove through it as if we were trained soldiers. Not that long ago, Liam and I had done something similar when we had to crawl through a shovel door in Grandpa Jake's silo to save a choking kitten's life.

Once Liam and I were through the gap, we knew exactly which direction to go because the no-no-bad-dog was baying like a beagle hot on a bunny trail.

When Liam and I paused at the fence separating the Fagan property from the uninhabited stable's next door, Ernest caught up with us. His face was beet-red, and beads of moisture dotted his cheeks.

"Go that way," he said, pointing to a gate halfway down the fence line. "I shouldn't know how to get to the old racing barn, but I do. A couple of years ago, Gramps had me climb through a broken window on the far end so I could retrieve a stall plaque from a favorite horse he used to ride when he was a child. That's hush-hush, though. If Aunt Cathy and Mom knew, Gramps and I would be in a whole lot of trouble."

I sprinted toward the gate, and for once, I got there before Liam. My adrenaline must be pumping full force into my bloodstream because I easily leaped over a giant log pile that was blocking the path like I was trotting my mount over *cavelettis,* also known as "ground poles."

"Wait up!" Ernest shouted. "I know an easier way to get inside the stable. If we circle around to the back, we can fit through a narrow door." Ernest swiped his forehead before abruptly turning right.

Liam and I stayed close to Ernest, cautiously following his footsteps across the barn's deterio- rating foundation. Once we were around the old wash-rack on the east side, we turned back toward the building.

Ernest pointed. "See the little door? It's tied shut with some old baler twine."

Liam being Liam asked, "How do you even know about this door if your grandpa had you go through a window on the front?"

Ernest flashed him a sideways grin. "Last summer, Gramps had me grab an old photo album that was in the office. He wanted pictures of my grandma and him from when they first started dating."

Hearing sweet stories like that reminded me of when my family had searched for a time capsule in Tennessee belonging to my friend, Kyle's grandfather.

Suddenly, we heard the most awful sound of crashing lumber—like the barn roof had collapsed. My stomach somersaulted, and seconds later, Sullivan yelped loudly in pain.

"Oh, no!" I shrieked. "We have to hurry. Something's happened to Sullivan."

 Liam yanked on the frayed twine securing the door. The harder he tried to untie the old rope, the tighter he pulled the knot. Frustrated, he exclaimed, "You try, Ernest! You're probably better at it than I am."

Ernest didn't waste time. He grabbed the tangled ends with each hand and tugged as hard as he could. Nothing happened!

"Quick, Liam! Use your jackknife! Cut it!"

Liam fished in his pocket for his prized possession. When he first wanted the silly pocketknife, I thought it was kind of stupid. Now, though, I couldn't imagine ever going anywhere without it. Between the knife, his fancy watch, and Mom's fanny pack, Liam and I had come out on top too many times to believe.

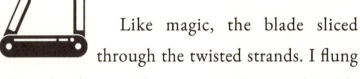 Like magic, the blade sliced through the twisted strands. I flung open the door, and as soon as I stepped inside the building, I started coughing. Hundred-year-old dust and debris saturated the place, making it difficult to breathe.

Liam grabbed my arm. "Wait, Mia! We need to cover our faces."

"With what?" I asked in a panic. "We have to quickly think of something, or I'm going in like I am."

Ernest shouted. "I've got it! Remember the package of bandanas Aunt Cathy had me stick in my back pocket when I couldn't stop sneezing?

Let's cover our faces with them like people used to do when Covid was bad."

"Great idea, Ernest!" Liam shouted. "That'll work!"

"Hurry!" I encouraged. "I'm worried about Sullivan. He hasn't made a sound since we first heard him cry."

Ernest tore at the plastic with his teeth. Liam and I snatched the red clothes out of the plastic before the bag was completely opened.

We quickly tied the checkerboard material over our nose and mouth.

"Which way?" Liam asked.

Ernest took the lead. "Straight ahead."

We found Sullivan in a standing stall next to the feed room. The closer we got to him, the more he whined.

He was lying down on his side, trapped under a maze of old wood and sheet metal. From where I was standing, I could only see a couple of superficial injuries, but I knew from working with Mom that he could have severe internal bleeding from blunt force trauma.

I saw that the end of his purple leash was precariously coiled around an old grain bag and several large posts. If they tumbled, we all could be seriously hurt. A large beam that was too heavy to lift stretched across the stall side-to-side near Sullivan's rear.

I slipped through the debris and settled by Sullivan's head. I wanted to reassure the poor pooch and check his gum color. Though it seemed like a lifetime ago, earlier this week, my family had rescued the Davidsons' Alaskan Malamute from the North Central State Trail. She had been injured by an angry black bear. While assisting Mom, she had reminded Liam and me how to check an animal's gums for signs of "shock."

Liam peered at me. "We can't get Sullivan out without removing this wooden beam. While Ernest and I try to move it, you stay by Sullivan's head and keep him calm."

Mom says you can tell a lot about an animal by looking at their eyes, but I couldn't tell if I saw fear or sadness in Sullivan's eye. I wished I had her gift for knowing how animals felt.

While the boys planned how to move the beam, I untied the fabric protecting my face and lungs and gently slid it under Sullivan's head to protect his face that was lying against the dirty floor. Because the cloth was long enough, I was able to use one corner to wipe away the dirt and debris collecting on his face.

"Mia, you shouldn't be breathing in this dust. Here, take my handkerchief. I'll pull my shirt off and tie it around my face like we saw people doing during the Lahaina fires. You need to protect yourself. Grab this!"

I took the bandana and tied it over my nose and mouth. *I love my smart and thoughtful brother.* We were a driven trio on a mission to save a beloved pet.

"Okay, Mia. Get ready. On the count of three, Ernest and I are going to lift this heavy beam that's trapping Sullivan. Your job is to move his hindquarters forward and to the side."

I barely heard what they were saying. All I could think about was how awful Sullivan had to be feeling. *I hope he doesn't have any broken bones.*

"One, two, three, Go!" Liam shouted.

I waited for the wood to move, for more dirt to fly our way, but nothing happened.

Ernest's voice sounded sad. "Poor Sullivan! Aunt Cathy is going to kill me if something happens to her dog."

Liam scratched his head. He thought for a moment than started looking around. He stepped outside the stall and momentarily returned with a long 2 x 4.

"What are you going to do with that?" Ernest asked. "I can't see how that's going to help our situation."

"Leverage," Liam said strutting toward Sullivan's rear with the 2 x 4 outstretched in front of him. He shoved the end of the 2 x 4 under the fallen beam and said, "Okay, Ernest, you and I are going to give this another try."

Sullivan whimpered, and I tried soothing him with my voice like Mom does when she sings lullabies to the young horses she has in training. This time when Liam said, "Go," I planned to use the extra bit of handkerchief to cover Sullivan's eyes so he wouldn't be as scared. I once saw a movie how a terrified horse had been blindfolded to be led out of a burning barn. *It can't hurt...*

Ernest held onto the end of the 2 x 4 where Liam directed. When they were ready, Liam started the countdown. I knelt closer to Sullivan's face, covered it with the bandana, then rested my head next to him. I gently blew into his nostrils, or what Mom refers to as *nares*, hoping it would be comforting. I had watched Mom do the same thing to a fractious young colt.

Please let Liam and Ernest get it this time.

"1, 2, 3, Go!" Liam shouted.

When I felt the smaller pieces of wood beside me move, my heart thumped even harder against my chest. *It's going to work. Liam is a genius!*

"I can't hold it any longer," Liam told Ernest. "We have to set it down. I just can't get enough leverage to raise the fallen beam high enough to free Sullivan."

My mind whirled. Focusing was hard with Sullivan whimpering. "Do it how a caveman would. Lean the 2 x 4 against something that's close to the ground."

"Mia!" Liam exclaimed. "Now isn't the time to be funny!"

"I'm not trying to be!" *Liam must think I'm poking fun at the not-so-smart thing he once said when we were visiting Mammoth Cave.*

"Like a fulcrum," Ernest shouted. "We learned about that in science class last year."

Liam's face lit up. "Duh!" he said. He tapped the side of his head with his hand. "Why didn't I think of that?"

Ernest touched Liam's arm. "We could use a cinder block from the pile we passed in the hallway on our way in. Stay where you are, and I'll go get one."

Ernest carefully stepped through the wood scraps littering the floor toward the exit.

Seconds later, he returned with a concrete block that was chipped at one end. "It'll still work." He wedged it under the base of the 2 x 4 Liam was holding.

Liam cracked a smile. "For good luck, let's skip the 1, 2, 3...."

Since Liam was taller than Ernest, he took his place closest the board's free end.

"Now," Liam directed.

Both boys tugged downward on the long piece of wood with all their strength until the 2 x 4 lowered enough for Liam to lay his chest across.

"You got it?" Ernest asked Liam.

Liam's face was deep red as he nodded.

Ernest slowly released his hold on the 2 x 4, then knelt to help me slide Sullivan's haunches forward. Once we were sure we had moved Sullivan far enough, Ernest stood back up and grabbed hold of the 2 x 4 to help Liam let it up slowly.

When Sullivan moved each of his back legs, I wanted to stand up and shout for joy. I hadn't wanted to admit to the boys, but the entire time the poor dog was trapped, I feared the beam had hit him with enough force to break his back, paralyzing poor Sullivan.

While Liam cleared the remaining scraps of wood and metal laying on the floor, I unsnapped the end of the long line that was attached to Sullivan's collar and handed it to Ernest. He untwisted the length of it before undoing its hold around the feed bags and discarded wood that was standing in the corner.

When the boys were finished and I was sure no more dust or debris could get in Sullivan's eyes, I carefully removed the protective handkerchiefs. Sullivan instantly rolled up on his sternum and before I realized what was happening, he planted a juicy, wet kiss on my cheek.

"Hooray!" Liam shouted.

"Here, Mia." Ernest said. "Now that Sullivan's leash is untangled, let's reclip him to the lead. I don't want him getting away again. Cat or no cat, if he tries that stunt another time, I'm holding on for dear life. He'll have to drag me behind him."

"Nice," Liam commented. "I can see it now. You'll be like a cowboy in an old western movie being dragged by his horse."

I glanced at Ernest, who despite Sullivan's drama, was smiling from ear to ear. "At least Ernest looks authentic wearing a bandana around his face like he's a bank robber."

"Good one, Mia," Liam said.

Sullivan suddenly stood up. "Wait, Buddy, I need to give you a quick exam."

 Like Mom had taught me, I lifted Sullivan's lip to check his gums. I knew they should normally be pink and moist, and they were. Next, I laid my hand on the left side of his chest behind his elbow to feel his heartbeat. "Liam, check your watch. Time me for 15 seconds."

Liam knew exactly what I was doing. He and I had helped Mom with small animal emergencies on the weekends so many times that we were comfortable taking vitals.

"Go." he said. "Stop!"

"Twenty-four," I said. "Let's do it again."

Liam gave me another fifteen seconds. "Stop!"

I removed my hand from Sullivan's side and gave him a big pat on the head. "Good boy! Twenty-three this time."

Like a math wizard, Liam replied, "That's 96 and 92. That's okay, right, Mia?"

"It sure is. A normal heartrate for a dog is around 100 beats per minute (bpm). Mom says it can vary though depending on the size of the dog and the situation."

I proceeded onward with my examination and carefully palpated all Sullivan's limbs. "I don't want to jinx the situation, but as hard as it is to believe, he only has a couple of scrapes."

Ernest's voice lifted. "That's fantastic. I was so worried."

Like they had been best friends forever, Liam slung his arm around Ernest's shoulders. "It wasn't your fault, Buddy. It could have happened to anyone."

"Quiet!" I said. "Did you hear that?" Liam and Ernest stopped talking and listened. I noticed Liam was covered in dirt from head to toe, and Ernest didn't look much better. "There it is again. Did you hear it? It's faint, but it sounds like kittens. Maybe that's why the cat Sullivan was chasing ran this way."

We stood absolutely still, waiting to hear the tiny meows. Even Sullivan seemed to understand and quit panting. With all the excitement, I hadn't realized how warm it was inside the building, and moisture saturated the front of my blouse. Like Liam and Ernest, my arms were covered in grime. "It sounds like they're close. Let's go see."

I peered down the old aisleway that was probably once the center of an active racehorse barn. Black leather harnesses covered with cobwebs hung on pegs beside me, and my first instinct was to reach out and touch the brittle leather. A sign on the door to my left said "Office," and a picture of a horse pulling a buggy hung on the wall beside it.

 Between the boards in the stall to my right, I noticed movement and took a tentative a step forward. While I watched, I motioned the boys forward. A long-haired orange kitten was playing with a length of baler twine dangling near the floor, and a dark-haired kitten, who looked more like a black puffball, was peeking out from the manger where it had been sleeping. The window on the sidewall above the manger was open, and a gentle breeze was blowing in.

"Let's go, Mia. They look old enough to be on their own."

 Liam was right. By their size and activity level, the kittens appeared to be at least six weeks old, and if the momma cat was too frightened to come back, they could survive. "Let me just close the window above the manger so they don't get rained on. Then we can leave."

"Hurry," Ernest begged. "It's bad enough I have to confess to Aunt Cathy what happened to Sullivan. I sure don't want to explain why we dilly-dallied in this abandoned stable any longer than we had to."

The instant I stepped into the stall, the young felines scampered. They reminded me of the feral kittens Liam and I had tried catching in Grandpa Jake's silo the previous summer. I was so deep in thought about Grandpa's farm, I didn't notice the irregularity of the damp, bumpy floor. Despite my normally good balance, I tripped.

I instinctively caught myself from falling by grabbing hold of the west, nasty windowsill. I suddenly noticed a thickly woven web with a giant spider glaring at me to the left of my hand. I hated spider webs but hated the yucky spiders that went with them even more.

Their long crinkly legs and arachnid bodies grossed me out. Sometimes, I even had nightmares about them.

That giant spider was all it took to kick me into high gear. *I am definitely ready to leave this old barn—NOW!* I reached up to pull down the window sash. The aged wood must have been swollen with moisture because it didn't want to budge.

Despite Mr. Spider's angry stare, I inched closer to the glass so I could get a better angle. With both hands in place, I pulled down as hard as I could. I was determined to make a rain-free environment for the kittens. But no matter how hard I pulled, the window wouldn't budge.

Just when I was about to give up, the window suddenly crashed downward. The abrupt movement carried years of dust and grime with it, and the upper stationary glass that had previously been covered with dirt was now clear to see through to the outside. What I saw did more than take my breath away.

"Ernest! Liam! Come quick and look!"

As good-natured as Ernest seemed to be, I could tell my request ruffled him. I knew we weren't supposed to be in these deserted stables, but I also knew I couldn't just pretend I hadn't seen what I just saw.

Ernest handed Sullivan's leash to Liam, then picked his way across the uneven floor toward me. Ernest wasn't as tall as me and for him to peek through the pane, he had to partially shimmy up the crusty wall. When he grasped the sill for support, his fingers came even closer to the thick web than mine had, and my neck hairs stood straight up.

I used the side of my hand to wipe off a lower section of glass for Ernest to peer through.

"Who's that, Ernest?" I asked. "And better yet, *how* did she get there?"

Standing fifty feet away from us under a maple tree next to a crumbling stone wall was a gorgeous cremello mare. Her creamy colored mane sifted in the soft wind before delicately landing on her creamy colored skin.

The pupils of Ernest's eyes widened like saucers. When he raised his eyebrows, his forehead disappeared beneath the bandana he was still wearing across his nose and mouth.

Liam hustled over. "What do you see? I wanna look."

Ernest yanked the handkerchief off his nose and mouth. "Surely the renters didn't abandon her a few weeks ago like they abandoned their cats?"

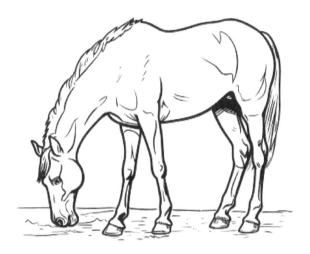

Glossary

A

Adrenaline - a hormone that is produced in the body in response to excitement, fear, or
stress. It
increases a person's breathing and heart rate.

Antihistamine - a medicine that inhibits histamine from being released. Treats allergic
reactions.

Arachnid - a wingless arthropod without antennae that has eight appendages. Includes
spiders, ticks, daddy longlegs, mites, and scorpions.

Artery - a blood vessel that transports blood away from the heart.

Asthma - bronchospasms and difficulty breathing. Often coughing and constricted feeling
to
chest.

B

Baying - a loud, long howl like a hound dog makes when on a scent.
Blood Vessel - a tubule in the body that carries blood.
Blunt Force Trauma - injury to the body because of forceful impact.
Bounding - strongly pulsing
BPM - refers to the heart. Beats-per-minute
Bronchiole - small tubule in lung that carriers oxygen.

C

Cadence - rhythmic, collected upward motion of horses hooves.
Cavelettis - poles on the ground or within six inches of ground that a horse trots over.
Canine - species name for dog.
Cremello - crème-colored horse with pale-white mane and tail. Blue eyes.
CRT - capillary Refill Time. Refers to amount of time it takes for mucous membranes
to
refill to normal pink color after they have been momentarily pressed on.
Currying - using a rubber or plastic type of brush often used to loosen dirt and mud.

D

Dam   - female parent of animal.

Digital Pulses - pulses palpated on sides of horses limb above the coronet band of hoof.

E

Equine   - species name for horse.

F

Feline   - species name for cat.

Flight Animals - a horse's first response to being frightened is to flee or run.

Forelock   - part of the mane on the horses forehead.

Foundered   - painful inflammation in horse's foot.

Fractious   - in veterinary medicine, an animal that is difficult to restrain.

Frog   - spongey V-shaped part of hoof.

Fulcrum   - a pivot point that a lever rests on.

H

Hand   - a four-inch incremental measurement used to determine height in horses.

Heels   - back most upper portion of hoof.

Hoof pick   - tool used to clean out a horse's hoof.

Hull   - main body of a boat.

I

Inhaler   - device used to deliver medicine to the lungs. Usually person inhales a
medication.

L

Leverage   - a way to lift heavy objects by using a long pole under the base for assistance.

Livetrap   - a cage that allows for capturing wild animals without harming them.

Locks   - a enclosed area that holds water that can be raised or lowered. Allows boats to
                       travel from level of water to another.

M

Mandible   - the lower portion of the jaw.

Muzzle   - the soft ending of a horses nose where the nostrils are locate.

N

Nares   - the end of the nostrils (the openings).

O

Oxygen Chamber   - a box or cage that is somewhat airtight allowing oxygen to concentrate and
                      make it easier for an animal to breathe.

P

Palpated   - toe use one's hands and fingers to examine an area.
Palpitated   - an unusual rhythm or speed to a person or animals heart.
Pinto   - a horse with splotches of white.
Plexiglass   - a heavy-duty see-through plastic.
Pollinating   - the transfer of pollen in a plant.
Porcine   - species name for a pig.
Prehensile   - term used to describe the delicate action a horse has with its lips to separate
food.

R

Radiograph   - another name for an x-ray.
Restraining   - word used to describe holding an animal usually for an examination.
Running board   - long step mounted to the frame of a truck to help a person getting in.

S

Saturate   - used in book to describe increasing to the greatest amount of oxygen in air.
Shy   - horse term to describe a horse becoming frightened by a noise, object, or
sound.
Sow   - mama pig.
Species   - scientific classification of animals with similar characteristics.
Stethoscope   - auditory device used to accentuate the sound of something like heart and lungs.
Sulci   - two grooves on either side of the frog in horse hoof
Sulcus   - one of the grooves on the side of the frog.

T

| Throatlatch | - describes the area on a horse between the mandible and base of ear. |
| Trailer Wraps | - horse bandages used to protect animals lower legs when trailering. |

W

| Withers | - highest point of horses back where it meets the neck. |

English Saddle Parts

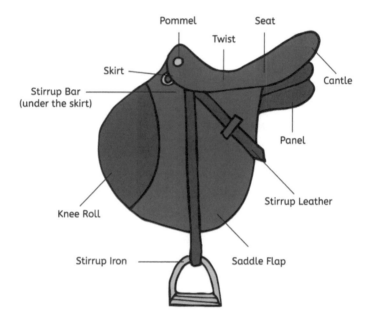

Parts of the horse

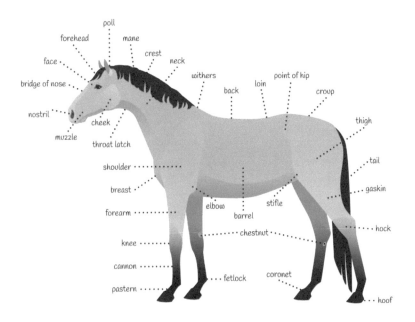

HORSE SKELETON

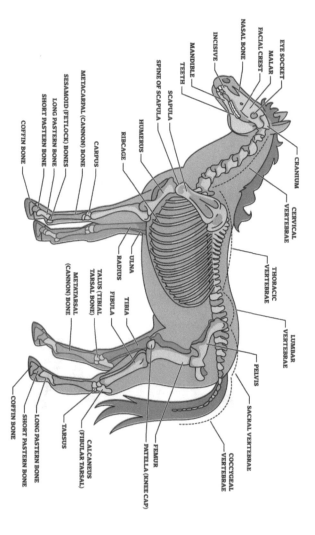

EYE SOCKET
MALAR
FACIAL CREST
NASAL BONE
INCISIVE
MANDIBLE
TEETH
SPINE OF SCAPULA
SCAPULA
HUMERUS
RIBCAGE
CARPUS
METACARPAL (CANNON) BONE
SESAMOID (FETLOCK) BONES
LONG PASTERN BONE
SHORT PASTERN BONE
COFFIN BONE

CRANIUM
CERVICAL VERTEBRAE
THORACIC VERTEBRAE
LUMBAR VERTEBRAE
PELVIS
SACRAL VERTEBRAE
COCCYGEAL VERTEBRAE
FEMUR
PATELLA (KNEE CAP)
CALCANEUS (FIBULAR TARSAL)
TARSUS
SHORT PASTERN BONE
LONG PASTERN BONE
COFFIN BONE
METATARSAL (CANNON) BONE
TALUS (TIBIAL TARSAL BONE)
FIBULA
TIBIA
ULNA
RADIUS

HORSE MUSCLES

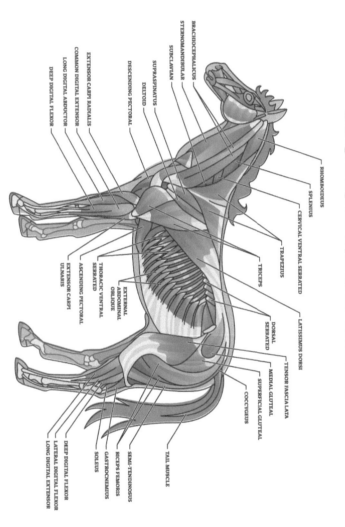

RHOMBOIDEUS
SPLENIUS
CERVICAL VENTRAL SERRATED
TRAPEZIUS
LATISSIMUS DORSI
TRICEPS
DORSAL SERRATED
TENSOR FASCIA LATA
MEDIAL GLUTEAL
SUPERFICIAL GLUTEAL
COCCYGEUS

BRACHIOCEPHALICUS
STERNOMANDIBULAR
SUBCLAVIAN
SUPRASPINATUS
DELTOID
DESCENDING PECTORAL
EXTENSOR CARPI RADIALIS
COMMON DIGITAL EXTENSOR
LONG DIGITAL ABDUKTOR
DEEP DIGITAL FLEXOR

EXTENSOR CARPI ULNARIS
ASCENDING PECTORAL
THORACIC VENTRAL SERRATED
EXTERNAL ABDOMINAL OBLIQUE

DEEP DIGITAL FLEXOR
LATERAL DIGITAL FLEXOR
LONG DIGITAL EXTENSOR
SOLEUS
GASTROCNEMIUS
BICEPS FEMORIS
SEMI-TENDINOSUS
TAIL MUSCLE

The

Vet Kids in Training
Equine Veterinary
Short Story
Learning Series

Are short stories
borrowed from:

The

Vet Kids Club
Chapter Books and Vet Kids
Horse Club learning Series

The following pages are examples from Aloha and the Mystery of the Runaway Pinto Activity Book which tests the reader's comprehension using FUN LEARNING ACTIVITIES

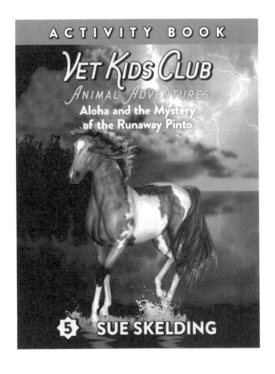

Help Mia and Liam find their way through the forest in search of a runaway pinto.

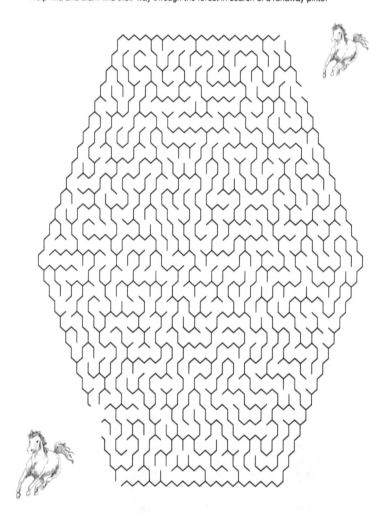

__ A __ __

L __ __ __

__ O __ __

__ __ __ __ H

__ __ A __ __ __ __

---

1. The Great Lake where the Edmund Fitzgerald sank.
2. A kind of artificial fishing bait.
3. Sharp pointed object on the end of a fishing line.
4. A type of fish often caught in the "flats" at Mullett Lake.
5. Mia's ling got _____ on the bottom of Mullett Lake.

Word Search: CITIES

E	F	D	V	B	B	D	V	M	O	M	P
T	M	S	D	F	U	B	M	I	T	F	T
A	L	O	H	A	C	K	H	R	E	V	X
T	C	V	D	S	K	O	H	E	W	S	R
S	Q	W	E	Z	E	T	S	G	H	L	E
E	L	T	R	I	Y	S	N	J	G	M	V
N	D	L	K	B	E	I	W	E	U	I	I
I	C	Z	Q	N	S	W	R	K	V	C	R
R	J	W	N	N	T	B	O	D	Y	H	N
E	D	E	A	S	A	W	B	I	G	I	A
V	T	L	S	P	T	Z	W	T	F	G	I
L	W	C	T	J	E	Q	K	G	I	A	D
O	Q	F	R	A	L	P	E	N	A	N	N
W	B	T	C	T	I	P	M	I	C	H	I

ACROSS	DOWN	DIAGONAL
ALPENA	INDIAN RIVER	TENNESSEE
ALOHA	WOLVERINE STATE	OHIO
	BUCKEYE STATE	
	MICHIGAN	

```
E               B           O
T               U       I
A   L   O   H   A   C       H       E
T               K   O       E               R
S               E       S   G               E
E               Y   S   N           M   V
N               E   I               I   I
I           N   S                   C   R
R       N   N   T                   H   N
E   E   A       A                   I   A
V T L           T                   G   I
L               E                   A   D
O           A   L   P   E   N   A   N   N
W                                       I
```

1. Lake
2. Lure
3. Hook
4. Perch
5. Snagged

Mia and Liam need your help!

If you **enjoyed** reading about Mia and Liam's animal experiences, I would be very appreciative if you could help other children also learn valuable veterinary information by:

1. Writing a **review** on Goodreads or Amazon books.

2. Upvote your favorite review that you read on Amazon. – All you need do is go to Amazon and **"like"** a review that's already posted.

3. Bring your book to school and share it with a classmate.

4. Show your librarian and ask her about the school purchasing the entire series.

5. Purchase a copy from Amazon or sueskeldingbooks.com and gift it to a friend.

VET KIDS CLUB
ANIMAL ADVENTURES
Veterinary chapter book learning series

VET KIDS HORSE CLUB
EQUINE ADVENTURES
Equine veterinary chapter book learning series

VKC ACTIVITY BOOKS

Join

Vet Kids Club Children's Facebook Group

Instructional Videos,
Proper Pet Care,
Laboratory Knowhow,
Exciting Radiographs,
Problem Solving, and
much more.

Questions:
skeldingsue@gmail.com

Sue Skelding graduated from veterinary school over thirty years ago. Her fondness for animals began as a young child on her grandfather's farm in Michigan where she was raised.

After Sue finished her first year of college in Grand Rapids, she moved to Colorado, where she completed her Doctor of Veterinary Medicine at Colorado State Veterinary Teaching Hospital. Sue then, moved back to lower Michigan where she built her first veterinary hospital.

Sue is currently a small animal veterinarian living and practicing in lower West Michigan. She Splits her free time between caring for her menagerie of animals, riding her horse, biking, and kayaking.

Love
Animals

Be Kind

To Others

Made in United States
Troutdale, OR
04/23/2024